# Youthful Leadership

NEHEMY N. KIHARA

Copyright © 2016 Nehemy Ndirangu Kihara, Ph.D.

All rights reserved.

ISBN: 1539544834
ISBN-13: **978-1539544838**

# DEDICATION

Dedicated to My Parish Mentor

the late Rev. Daniel Gitogo Githanji and

to my Presbyterial colleagues,

the late Rev .John Thuo and Rev. Jason Nyaga;

To all the young leaders of Africa and the rest of the Globe.

The future World will be predominantly Youthful,

We also dedicate this book to them.

Dedicated to all the Elderly,

that are always Youthful in Mind and Spirit,

their leadership and guidance is highly appreciated.

# CONTENTS

|   | Acknowledgments | i |
|---|---|---|
| 1 | Introduction | 1 |
| 2 | Theoretical Consideration | 3 |
| 3 | Motivation for Leadership | 6 |
| 4 | Leadership Behavior | 10 |
| 5 | Behavior Indicators | 14 |
| 6 | Style Settings | 19 |
| 7 | Situational Determinants | 26 |
| 8 | Alternative Youthful Leadership | 30 |
| 9 | Conclusive Remarks | 33 |
| 10 | References | 38 |

# ACKNOWLEDGMENTS

My acknowledgements go to the
Presbyterian Church of East Africa, for
having accepted me at the age of 18 to train for the Ministry..
Acknowledgements are given also to
the Tumutumu Presbytery /Nanyuki Parish
for recommending me, against previous traditions(teenagers were not
allowed for theological training).
Acknowledgements also go to Murang:a Presbytery,
for Licensing me at the age of 21 yrs., before
Ordaining me at the age of 22 yrs., and .for choosing me the
Presbytery Clerk and Presbyterial Youth Minister.
Acknowledgements also
and to all members of Muthithi Parish for having accepted me ,
the youngest Minister in the Presbyterian Church of East Africa,
as their Moderator and Youthful Leader.

# 1 INTRODUCTION

Leadership should be interpreted as a relationship that exists between persons in a social setting or situation.

As such a person may be a leader in some situation and necessarily not be one in another (Stogdill: 1974).

The reason for this, is because certain qualities are required for leadership over a particular group ; for an example;. women, children or youth activities.

Therefore, an employee such as a Departmental Office messenger can be suitable for a church leadership role while their boss - the H.O.D. (Head of Department) is just a member with no leadership role in the same Church.

Influencing the action of others is the essence of leadership and leaders must be people with a conviction for things that need to be done and have the ability to persuade others to join them in getting things done. That is an essential quality of leadership.

Another essential quality of leadership especially for the Christian Church is the servant/shepherd model of Jesus Christ - considering that followers are potential leaders, who constantly need discipline and developing.

# 2 THEORETICAL CONSIDERATION: SOCIAL PSYCHOLOGY

There has been a great deal of social psychological research on leadership.

Four of the findings seem worthy our consideration:

1. Leadership is partly situational and partly intrinsic to the person.

In other words, there are a few individuals who are accepted as leaders in many all situations, but there are whose leadership may be accepted in a number of situations, because of abilities that are relevant to the situation.

2. In most groups there are two leadership roles.

(a) the task of a leader who organizes the group for actions.

(b)the maintenance leader who through his/her empathy and good humor, keeps the group in a state of emotional equilibrium.

3. In task oriented groups the leader who is concerned with both the achievement of the group tasks and the well-being of the group members tends to be more effective than the one who is only tasks oriented or oriented only to the needs of group members.

4. There is a greater commitment to the group task, greater attention, and greater self-reliance in the members democratically led groups than groups with autocratic or laisse-faire leaders.

According to Fielders (1964) early research, the leader who is detached enough to have preferences among workers is more effective than the one who prefers not to feel differentially toward subordinates.

His further work on the contingency model of leadership; however suggests that the interpersonally oriented leader.

This leader who does not like to discriminate between workers tends to be quite successful in raising group performance in task situations that are moderately favorable to him or every unfavorable to him, the discriminating task-oriented leader is likely to be needed to raise group performance.

Fieldler considers a task situation as favorable to the leader if the leader is well liked by subordinates if the group task is structured and group performance is quantifiable, and if the leader has considerable positional and expertise based authority.

A task situation is considered to be unfavorable if the leader is disliked, if the group task is ambiguous and if the leader does not have much authority over subordinates.

# 3 MOTIVATION FOR LEADERSHIP

There has been a great deal of social psychological research on leadership.

Four of the findings seem worthy our consideration:

1. Leadership is partly situational and partly intrinsic to the person.

In other words, there are a few individuals who are accepted as leaders in many all situations, but there are whose leadership may be accepted in a number of situations, because of abilities that are relevant to the situation.

2.In most groups there are two leadership roles.

(a)the task of a leader who organizes the group for actions.

(b)the maintenance leader who through his/her empathy and good humor, keeps the group in a state of emotional equilibrium.

3.In task oriented groups the leader who is concerned with both the achievement of the group tasks and the well-being of the group members tends to be more effective than the one who is only tasks oriented or oriented only to the needs of group members.

4.There is a greater commitment to the group task, greater attention, and greater self-reliance in the members democratically led groups than groups with autocratic or laissen-faire leaders.

Fielder's (1964) early research, suggested that the leader who is detached enough to have preferences among workers is more effective than the one who prefers not to feel differentially toward subordinates.

His further work on the contingency (situational) model of leadership; however suggests that the interpersonally oriented leader is more efficient. Most of the situational theories developed in the 1960s and 1970s; argued that factors of each situation determine the effectiveness of behavior.

The interpersonally oriented leader does not like to discriminate between workers tends to be quite successful in raising group performance in task situations that are moderately favorable to him or every unfavorable to him, the discriminating task-oriented leader is likely to be needed to raise group performance.

Fieldler considers a task situation as favorable to the leader if the leader is well liked by subordinates if the group task is structured and group performance is quantifiable, and if the leader has considerable positional and expertise based authority.

A task situation is considered to be unfavorable if the leader is disliked, if the group task is ambiguous and if the leader does not have much authority over subordinates.

# 4 LEADERSHIP BEHAVIOR

Virtually three types of leadership behaviors or styles have been identified:-

1. Authoritarian ; always defensive, fears others; distrusts, thrives on disinformation or distorted information, uses strategies of persuasion; such as claiming outside attack.

2. Democratic - always participatory, trusts others, have confidence, task oriented, perceives other human beings as responsible.

3. Laissez-faire-individual activities allowed without interference or control.

Likert (1961) citing evidence from research, indicated that managers in government are the most effective in achieving superior performance.

While the managers in business who achieve the highest productivity and best employee cooperation and management were those who built the subordinates into a cohesive, highly effective cooperative problem solving teams.

Stogdill (1974) however, does not support any supervisory role. At least two supervisory - leadership ideal types are notable.

1. Those who easily seem to function more comfortably and naturally as highly directive leaders, thereby, issues orders easily and are tasks-oriented.

2. Those who operate more comfortably in team work, thereby sharing many of their functions with their subordinates and are relations oriented.

Surgiovanni and Elliot (1975) have come up with what they call the leadership grid, with both a task (horizontal margin axis) and people (vertical marginal axis) dimensions.

Basically, the grid is defined by the extent to which a leader seems to show concern for, focuses on, or seems oriented toward getting work done or accomplishing task - task oriented (TO); and the extent to which the leader seem to show concern for, focuses on, or seems oriented the needs or feelings of people and his/her relationships with them - relations oriented (R.O.).

Simply, to find your location in the grid, based on the estimates you have made, simply find the point where lines drawn from each of the numbers you checked would intersect. For example, if you checked a 6 on the - T.O. line and 7 on the R.O. line your position on the grid would be indicated by the X which appears on the grid.

Reddin (1970) 3-D theory assumes that no one leadership style exists. He developed quadrants.

1. Dedicated style - lower - right hand (to high and Ro low) emphasis on work and little overt concern for the relationship dimension.

2. Related style - upper - left hand (To low and RO high) emphasis on people and littler overt concern for the task dimension.

3. Integrated style - upper-right hand (TO high and RO high) characterized by combined approach to supervision, peoples, concerns, expressed through emphasis on meaningful work and work concerns emphasized by bringing together and stimulating committed groups of individuals.

4. Separated style - lower - left hand (To low and Ro low) expresses very little concern for either dimension. Leader removes him/herself from both tasks and people.

From the four managerial style 8 more behavior styles are formed..

| Basic Style | Less Effective Managerial Style | More Effective Managerial Style |
|---|---|---|
| Separated | Deserter | Bureaucrat |
| Related | Missionary | Developer |
| Dedicated | Autocrat | Benevolent Autocrat |
| Integrated | Compromiser | Executive |

Along the x/y axis of T.O. and R.O. is the interplay of D.O.(Dimensionality of Effectiveness).

# 5 BEHAVIOR INDICATORS

The basic leadership style behavior indicators, could be described in several ways. There is a relationship between the three basic communication styles with the way one tends to lead others;

1. Aggressive

2. Passive

3. Assertive

When one examines the four basic decision making styles of;

1. Authoritative

2. Consultative

3. Facilitative

4. Delegative

Each of these style will at time tend to go with specific communication styles, However most results are achieved through being assertive leadership, that is equipped with proper knowledge and information.

In a developing and democratizing society, authoritative leaders must ensure that they their experience is backed up by more information and expertise than the people they lead.

Mostly the skills needed to lead and manage are to listen, interact, accept, motivate, trust, integrate, advice ,participate, encourage and to innovate.

Leaders also need skills to examine, organize, measure, initiate, administer, direct, control, complete, maintain, and evaluate.

Further, William James Reddin (1970) 3-dimensional theory of leadership develops into :two types of managerial behaviors- Task Orientation (TO) or Relationship Orientation(RO).,that determine Managerial Effectiveness, mostly contingent on the situation.

The basic assumptions are that managers are either concerned with getting tasks done (TO) or with the relationships of people (RO)

Dedicated Managers-more Task Oriented style.

Related Managers-more Relationship Oriented style.

Separated Managers-less T.O. and less R.O. Style

Integrated Managers- use both R.O. and T.O. together.

# 6 STYLE SETTINGS

The three classical definitions of leadership styles have been :

1. Autocratic- where the leader makes all decisions without consulting.

2. Laissez-faire , freewheeling or hands-off.-where decisions are left to all Laissez-faire or hands -off freewheeling or o implement.

3. Participative, or democratic-where decisions are reached through sharing and consultations.

The other 4 ways of defining leadership styles are;

1. Situational Leadership doing what the situation demands.

2. Transactional Leadership, doing what is acceptable to the institution or industry.

3. Transformational Leadership, this means that one tries different ways of doing things.

4. Strategic Leadership, this is marked by proper thinking and planning ways before doing things

The other 6 ways of defining leadership styles, that are popular in management psychology are;

1. Commanding or coercive leadership that demands compliance.

2. Pacesetting, leading the way to be followed

3. Democratic, consensus and participation

4. Affliative, creating feelings of membership and belonging

5. Coaching, developing teamwork

6. Authoritative or Visionary, creating vision and common goal for leadership.

Most of the authoritative government thrive on passive followers and a direct leader who is more experience the ,as the only source of information and by that virtue the experts in societal management.

In contrast most of the youth in the information age, equally possesses information and expertise necessary to manage the modern society.

Therefore, the need for less consultative management strategy. As opposed to the facilitative leadership in which they share all tasks and arrive at shared decision.

Furthermore, we still have to wait for Governments who use delegate decision where bureaucratic manager delegates tasks and followers make decisions.

# YOUTHFUL LEADERSHIP

In Kenya, the founding father Jomo Kenyatta, had created a very professional leadership, which transformed the country from a colonial post, to a modernizing state, with one of the best economic performance in Eastern Africa.

It was not long before he become a benevolent autocrat who knew what he wanted and how to get it without creating a lot of resentment.

However, that was short-lived because as he grew older he seemed to have become a repressive autocrat, who had lost confidence in other leaders in his cabinet.

The one party dominated Government of the day became more forceful in getting people to do what it wanted. Many of the policy decisions were poorly made, due to unnecessary pressure and influence .

Kenya as country had good leaders in many other sectors who set high standards in their institutions and kept society holding together, until the death of Kenyatta.

His Vice President Daniel Moi, took over who immediately behaved like the missionary the African Inland Mission had created in him. He was a mission teacher before getting into politics.

Moi leadership of the nation, started with a lot of people viewing him as a passing compromiser, who lacked the forceful leadership of Kenyatta; but he immediately proved to be a good developer and motivator, interested in harmony.

However in the final days of his almost a quarter of a century as the President of Kenya, he created a lot of resentments, he had moved from a benevolent to a repressive autocrat following the 'nyayo' (Swahili for footsteps) of Kenyatta.

# YOUTHFUL LEADERSHIP

Mwai Kibaki, a former Vice -President under Moi ,become the President in a multi-party election. He served two terms, before being replaced by the son of Jomo Kenyatta, Uhuru Kenyatta, predicated to win and serve a send term.

Kibaki and Uhuru are said to have been less forceful in their leadership styles. In comparison with Mzee Kenyatta and Moi who at one time had become forceful autocrats.

# 7 SITUATIONAL DETERMINANTS

Youth is a social fact rather than biological. Virtually by the end of teenage - between 18 and 19 years; anyone is physiologically an adult, having reached sexual maturity and the peak of physical and mental capacity.

The idea of youth as a stage of life, therefore follows both childhood which ends at 13 years and adolescence (between age 13 to 16). But it is prior to full time participation in work roles (probably ages 16 to 21 or to 25). In some general terms youth is defined as those between age 15/16 to 35.

As such, we can say that youth have always been there in history, but today a large proportion of our population is youthful'.

However, there is no biological imperative to reinforce the idea that after puberty young people should be categorized or segregated from adults by being prevented from assuming adult sexual, economic and political roles.

In most of African cultures or ethnic communities, children were mixed with adults immediately after waning around age seven. These were taught roles they had to assume by the period they enter into initiation ceremonies around puberty-which was a necessary transitional experience.

The stage of separation was not independent of adult or older generation, nor was it permanent, but an ongoing process of growth toward adulthood. Generational relations were therefore, characterized by equilibrium rather than conflict.

The segregation and categorization of young people in a contemporary situation can be seen as a result of an increasingly complex, differentiated, industrialized and bureaucratized culture.

In the past decade African societies have experienced a pattern of change that has threatened the stability of cultural framework, which in the indigenous setting provided the youth with a sense of purpose, meaning and confidence.

The emergence of this sort of societal convulsion and the emergence of youth revolt or revolution; has created a situation in which young people distrust and even have contempt for organizations that are identified with the establishment.

As a result the young people have responded to the experience not as "youth" or women but as people - workers, farmers or students.

African societies have experienced extensive militant protests and rebellions, but rarely if ever has such activity been carried on by those who define themselves as "the youth" (even when many of those who have been active in such struggles have tended to be young).

While most of the current political systems seem repressive, unjust and corrupt; with deep political and economic problems that generate resentment and wide discontent; collective youthful' responses also expected, seems turbulent and unpredictable.

# 8 ALTERNATIVE YOUTHFUL LEADERSHIP

As Africa gets deeper into the era of democratization, more accountable and transparent leadership will be required. Retrogressive, absolute and incoherent ideological politics backed by autocratic and authoritarian governance have created deeply entrenched problems.

These have complicated more by offering only empty promises of solutions. As we move into the next three decades in the Millennium (towards A.D. 2030), in there is a feeling that no leadership that exists today in Africa can solve our historical crisis.

During the four decades into the new 21 st century ; the generation capable of making that transformation (fundamentally social and cultural) has already been produced – the ' youthful' ones.

We have already witnessed in the middle of second decade of AD. 2000, that in many countries the process of change has been and will be painful, chaotic and even bloody.

Many of the remarkable protest in Ethiopia are organized and carried out by young people from the Oromo and Amhara communities who have been complaining of oppressive governance by the minority Tigrinya regime that exclusively controls the country.

There has been complaints of the central government encroaching into the lands that belongs to those communities, near the capital city of Addis Ababa.

The response of the government forces to these protests have been more less brutal. In other capitals in Africa similar protests against governments that seem rather oppressive and unresponsive to the needs of its citizens, seem to attract young people, including some attending primary/elementary schools.

In some countries there has been complaints about school riots. organized and carried by the young ones.

Unfortunately, some of the youth in Africa seem to be reaffirming their ethnic identities and the rights of their linguo-ethnic communities as opposed to the collective, trans-ethnic nationalism or Pan-Africanism.

Just being biologically young however, does not necessary mean that one is going to be a good leaders as witnessed by such ruthless Presidents of Liberia-Doe and his successor Taylor.

What matters is the mindset of mindset of 'youth', which is marked by experimental spirit, freshness, energy and renewal. Old age is characterized by baggages of everyday hussles that come with long life as well experience and wisdom. Both leaderships are needed in societal management and development.

## 9 CONCLUSIVE REMARKS

As agents of social change beyond AD 2030, the youth will be suited and developed for a leadership that is more responsive to the aspirations and demands of the people to be what the Creator God intended them to be, free, creative, less materialistic and cooperative.

The 'youthful' culture that will be needed have to advocate a more open society, with new hopes, expectations, fulfilment and capable of humanizing technology.

Most of the influential leaders had much of their impact during their 'youthful ' period. Some in their thirties include Jesus Christ and one of his later day disciples Rev. Dr. Martin Luther King, Jr.(proponent of the non-violence approach to social change and civil rights leader).

Therefore, the servant/shepherd model of leadership exemplified by Jesus Christ need to be given special attention., especially in regard to Church or Christian leadership. While certain qualities are required for leadership over particular groups; the quality of ,emphathy, love and compassion if applicable in all groups.

The leadership model by Jesus, helps us to develop others through discipleship to become leaders. The followers of Jesus, namely his disciples became leaders to carry on his ministry ( Yousseff, 1986).

The recognition of the potentiality of leadership in those that are being led or the followers, requires that we became flexible, sensitive to others and interdependent.

The diversified ministry of the Church offers situations in which nobody ought to be excluded from leadership based on the lack of certain personality traits, recognized by the business or industrial standards as essential.

The objectives of African nations or all developing countries are, to socially and economically develop. That entails building viable institutions to meet the basic human needs. People need to have energy for lighting, cooking and keeping them warm. Or even to cool them (in the case of air conditioning)

These organizational objectives; require effective leadership skills; to attain the set goals for the development process at least at the minimum satisfaction. Any societal or National Development requires management. These will be able to utilize the (P.O.L.C.) principles of management translated into the critical functions of Planning, Organizing, Leading and Coordinating.

When teaching courses in Security Management and Police Studies, for the now Department of Security and Correctional Science, Kenyatta University, Nanyuki, Nyeri and Embu Campuses; it occurred to me that these same principles define what effective, community based and intelligence led policing is supposed to be.

Furthermore, proper efficient P.O.L.I.C.E.- should be well skilled in **P**lanning, **O**rganizing, **L**eadership, Information/Intelligence, **C**oordinating and **E**nforcing. These principles must guide every Police Force, that needs to utilize sound management and skills utilization of its formation.

Most of the mismanagement and misuse of resources, have come because of the 'older' assumption that all we need is good managers, but experience has taught us that we need management with leadership and development skills.

While these skills may not be available in one individuals, we should then be able to utilize all the people we have regardless of or rankings, within the organization.

Managers work on everyday implementation, controlling financial and other resources necessary to achieve the goals are to be reached. But leaders are the ones with the know-how, who motivate people and have the skills of getting goals implanted.

While developers implement the process of these goals implementation. Leaders are the ones who know what need to be done to get to the goals and motivates people to get there.

# 10 REFERENCES

1. Argyris, Chris (1957). Personality and Organization. N.Y.: Harper and Row.

2. Dublin, Robert (1974). Human Relations in Administration with Readings 4th ed. N.J.: Prentice-hall.

3. Fiedler, F.E. (1967). A Theory of Leadership Effectiveness. New York: -Hill.

4. Gibb, Jack R. (1967). "Dynamics of Leadership in Search of Leaders." Washington D.C. National Education Association.

5. Herberzburgh, F. (1966). Work and the Nature of Woman. Cleveland: World.

6. Kaplan, H.R. and Kurt Tausky (1977)."Humanism in Organization: A Critical Appraisal Public Administration Review.

7. Likert, Rennis (1961). New Patterns of Management. New York.

8. Maslow, Abraham H. (1970). Motivation and Personality 2nd ed. N.Y.: Harper and Row.

9. Reddin, William J. (1970). Management Effectiveness, N.Y.: McGraw-Hill.

10. Sergiovannieddin, Thomas J. (ed.) (1975). Educational and Organization: Leadership in Elementary Schools.

11. Stogdill, Ralph M. (1974). Handbook of Leadership; A Survey of Theory and Research. N.Y.: Free Press.

12. Strauss, George (1974). "Workers: Attitudes and Adjustments" in Jerome M. Rosow (ed.). The Worker and the Job: Coping with Change. Englewood Cliffs, N.J.: Prentice-Hall.

13. Youssef, Michael (1986). The Leadership Style of Jesus. US.; Victor Books.

# ABOUT THE AUTHOR

The Revd. Prof. Dr. Nehemy Ndirangu Kihara was born in Nanyuki in Laikipia County of Kenya, East Africa.

He was educated at Timau in Meru County and Nairobi before graduating with a Licentiate of Theological Education from St. Paul's University (United Theological College), Limuru in Kiambu County.

He holds a Bachelor of Theology (B.Th.) in Biblical Literature and Geographic History from Christian International College.

As an Investigative Journalist and Radio Broadcaster this Independent Publisher hosted a weekend English and still hosts a weekly Swahili Community Show for Sagal Radio Services at WATB 1420 AM Station in Decatur, GA.

As an Interdisplinary Educator he taught Security Management and Police Studies for the Institute of Peace and Security Studies, (now known as the Department of Security and Correctional Science) of Kenyatta University in Nanyuki Campus, where he was the Coordinator of Humanities and Examinations Officer.

The Author also taught Introductory Psychology, Sociology, Criminal Procedure and Law of Evidence, Intelligence-Led Policing, Public Administration and General Management Principles among other units at the Nyeri and Embu Campuses.

He was an Adjunct Professor of Sociology/ Social Sciences at the Atlanta Campus of Saint Leo University, Tampa, Fl. Taught such courses as Anthropology, Sociology, and Criminal Justice units as Social Theory, Drugs and Society, Marriage and Family, Research Methods, Human Behavior, among others He was an Adjunct Professor of Ethics at the Georgia Campus (Henry Medical Center) of the College of Health, University of St. Francis, Joliet, Ill.,

The Author was also the founding Moderating Bishop of the Ujamaa Nomadic Church -Without Borders, as a new church- mission initiative in US. He had also been an Urban Renewal/ Organizing Pastor of Beth Salem United Presbyterian Church, Columbus, Georgia. He served as an International Missionary in California, Iowa and New York, under the Mission to US program of the Presbyterian Church, USA.

As a Senior Lecturer at Kenyatta University, the Author taught African Culture, Belief Systems, Social Theory and Research Methods units in the Department of Philosophy and Religious Studies and also in the Department of Sociology. He was also an Activist Educator, who fought for academic freedom and excellence, which led to his unfair dismissal by the government which controlled the public universities and educational institutions.

Reverend Professor Ndirangu Kihara started his career a high school teacher and principal at Muthithi Secondary School, and then an ordained Church Minister of Muthithi Parish and the Stated Clerk of the wider Murang'a Presbytery of the Presbyterian Church of East Africa.

NEHEMY N. KIHARA

BLUERGREEN PUBLISHING